Central Skagit Sedro-Woolley Library
802 Ball St.
Sedro-Woolley WA 98284
Jan 2019

INSIDE THE
DEPARTMENT OF
Homeland Security

Jennifer Peters

Enslow Publishing
101 W. 23rd Street
Suite 240
New York, NY 10011
USA
enslow.com

Published in 2019 by Enslow Publishing, LLC
101 W. 23rd Street, Suite 240, New York, NY 10011

Copyright © 2019 by Enslow Publishing, LLC

All rights reserved.

No part of this book may be reproduced by any means without the written permission of the publisher.

Library of Congress Cataloging-in-Publication Data

Names: Peters, Jennifer, author. | Haulley, Fletcher, author.
Title: Inside the Department of Homeland Security / Jennifer Peters, Fletcher Haulley.
Description: New York : Enslow Publishing, 2019. | Series: Understanding the executive
  branch | Includes bibliographical references and index. | Audience: Grades 5-8.
Identifiers: LCCN 2017060609 | ISBN 9780766098930 (library bound) | ISBN
  9780766098947 (pbk.)
Subjects: LCSH: United States. Department of Homeland Security—Juvenile literature. |
  Terrorism—United States—Prevention—Juvenile literature. | National security—United
  States—Juvenile literature.
Classification: LCC HV6432.4 .P47 2019 | DDC 363.340973—dc23
LC record available at https://lccn.loc.gov/2017060609

Printed in the United States of America

To Our Readers: We have done our best to make sure all website addresses in this book were active and appropriate when we went to press. However, the author and the publisher have no control over and assume no liability for the material available on those websites or on any websites they may link to. Any comments or suggestions can be sent by email to customerservice@enslow.com.

Portions of this book originally appeared in *The Department of Homeland Security* by Fletcher Haulley.

Photo Credits: Cover, p. 1 quavondo/Getty Images; pp. 5, 20 New York Daily News Archive/Getty Images; p. 8 Spencer Platt/Getty Images; p. 9 Bettmann/Getty Images; p. 11 AFP/Getty Images; p. 15 Karen Bleier/AFP/Getty Images; p. 17 Getty Images; p. 19 Hulton Archive/Archive Photos/Getty Images; p. 23 Mark Wilson/Getty Images; p. 25 Don Emmert/AFP/Getty Images; pp. 27, 28, 33 Paul J. Richards/AFP/Getty Images; p. 30 Jose Jimenez/Primera Hora/Getty Images; p. 34 Drew Angerer/Getty Images; p. 36 Bloomberg/Getty Images.

CONTENTS

INTRODUCTION

One of the newest cabinet departments is the Department of Homeland Security. Created after the September 11, 2001, terror attacks on New York's World Trade Center and the Pentagon near Washington, DC, the department's primary objective is to keep Americans safe within the borders of the United States.

Nearly three thousand people were killed that day, and it was immediately clear that something needed to be done to prevent future attacks.

At the time, while many intelligence agencies had bits of information that would have helped stop the attacks, the agencies rarely shared information. President George W. Bush believed it was necessary to create an office that would facilitate the sharing of information. Within weeks of the September 11 attacks, the Office of Homeland Security was created to fill this void, and nine months later, it was promoted to a cabinet-level department.

The Department of Homeland Security was created with three specific purposes in mind: to prevent terrorist attacks within the United States, to reduce America's vulnerability to terrorism, and to minimize the damage and speed the recovery from attacks that do occur. The department does not serve a brand-new purpose. There have always been government agencies working to defend the United States and its citizens

The terrorist attacks on September 11 made homeland security a priority for the United States.

from attacks at home and abroad. Rather, the new department brings together under one roof many agencies of the government that already exist, helping to create a more unified effort.

The terrorist attacks of September 11 highlighted the need for a reorganization of the US government. However, before sweeping new powers could be granted to the US government to fight terrorist threats, the often-troubled history of homeland security had to be reviewed and a plan needed to be made that would strike the right balance between law and order on one side and freedoms and civil liberties on the other. American responses to domestic threats have often gone beyond the legal limits imposed on the government by the US Constitution. Both private citizens and immigrants have occasionally been unjustly denied their guaranteed rights and freedoms during times of heightened national security. It is the very difficult job of the Department of Homeland Security to protect citizens from attack while also safeguarding their personal freedoms, the very freedoms upon which the United States was founded.

CHAPTER 1

HOMELAND SECURITY'S COMPLICATED HISTORY

Prior to the September 11, 2001, terrorist attacks, the United States had experienced very few attacks on its soil. That's in large part because the United States is so far from the countries it has been in conflict with. The Pacific Ocean separates America from Asia, while enemies from Europe would have to cross the Atlantic Ocean to attack. While brief skirmishes with Mexico in the mid-1800s did pop up, the threat of war on American soil was minimal. Even the Japanese bombing of Pearl Harbor in Hawaii on December 7, 1941, was a long-distance attack on a US military installation on an island thousands of miles from the American mainland.

The Freedom Tower, built on the spot of the World Trade Center, has increased security.

The Japanese attack on Pearl Harbor was the first attack on American soil in over a century and the last until September 11, 2001.

A threat to national security usually comes from a specific group of people. For example, the September 11 hijackers were all Islamic radicals, and many of them were from Saudi Arabia. Because of this, specific groups are often targeted in the name of homeland security, which raises some difficult questions. What should the United States do with immigrants from hostile countries living within its borders? Do they still have the rights guaranteed to American citizens in the Constitution? Or does the safety of the larger population merit taking away the rights of this smaller group? These are questions that the United States has faced every time there has been a threat to national security.

PROFILING

During World War II, America found itself with what it perceived to be a major problem. At the time of the attack on Pearl Harbor and the United States' declaration of war against Japan, well over one hundred thousand Japanese Americans lived on the West Coast of the United States. President Franklin D. Roosevelt's administration, the US Congress, and many American citizens feared that these Japanese Americans (many of whom were born in the United States and were full citizens) would remain more loyal to the land of their ancestry than to America.

The possibility that these people might arm themselves in the name of Japan and attack the US government was extremely unlikely. For the most part, these immigrants had escaped poverty and repression in Japan to find freedom and opportunity in America. Their faith in the United States was rewarded during wartime by having their freedom taken away. More than 120,000 Japanese Americans were forced out of their homes and interned— or imprisoned—in camps throughout the

During World War II, Japanese American citizens were held in camps and often forced to do labor.

POLICING AMERICA'S BORDERS

The Department of Homeland Security became responsible for administering the nation's immigration laws on March 1, 2003, when the Immigration and Naturalization Service (INS) became part of the department. Among the department's many duties is immigration enforcement, which includes preventing immigrants from entering the country unlawfully; finding and removing those who are living in the United States unlawfully; and preventing terrorists and other criminals from entering or living in the United States. The Department of Homeland Security tries to strike a balance between welcoming law-abiding visitors and immigrants and identifying and keeping out possible terrorists.

American West. For several years, they were not allowed to leave these barbed-wire compounds. When they returned to their homes after the war, new families were living in them and their businesses had long since gone bankrupt. The Japanese Americans were treated as if they had committed treason and were forced to pay the price for it. The rights of Japanese Americans were severely abused in the name of domestic security. To this day, Japanese internment remains one of the most shameful episodes in American history.

Many people argue that increased homeland security always means that citizens must give up some of their rights and freedoms. Indeed, throughout American history that has often been the case. Often the groups suspected of anti-American activities are composed of recent immigrants. All immigrants from these particular ethnic groups then become suspect, regardless of their political beliefs. Immigrants often are not yet allowed to vote and therefore have little influence with politicians and the government. They usually come to America for work because they cannot support their families in their own countries. They lack the money to hire lawyers or lobbyists to help defend themselves against attempts by the government to limit their rights and freedom. This is what Japanese Americans faced in the 1940s, and many Muslim Americans are now facing a similar situation.

HOMEGROWN TERROR

Terrorism has long been a security concern for the United States, but it was not always its main concern. Until September 11, 2001, the majority of terrorist attacks directed against Americans occurred outside of the United States. In 1998, for example, al-Qaeda, the terrorist network responsible for the September 11 attacks, blew up the American embassies in Nairobi, Kenya, and Dar es Salaam, Tanzania. The bombings, which occurred within minutes of each other, killed 224 people, most of whom were Africans. In response, the president at the time, Bill Clinton, fired several cruise missiles at al-Qaeda chief Osama bin Laden's training camps in Afghanistan. The missiles hit the camp but missed their

Americans have also been behind terrorist acts, like the Oklahoma City bombing.

real target, bin Laden. In 2000, bin Laden delivered his retaliation by bombing the USS *Cole* in a harbor in Yemen, killing seventeen sailors.

Terrorism has actually reached American soil a few times, however. In 1996, an antigovernment American terrorist named Timothy McVeigh blew up a federal building in Oklahoma City, Oklahoma, killing 168 people. Another homegrown terrorist who plagued the United States from the late 1970s through the 1990s was Ted Kaczynski, known as the Unabomber. Kaczysnki was a mentally ill individual who developed a deep hatred of technology and lived in primitive solitude in rural Montana. To protest the modern world, he sent bombs by mail to scientists, academics, and executives of major corporations. Several people were killed by these mail bombs, and many were severely injured.

Another example of terrorism as protest is found in the late 1960s and early 1970s, with a student group called the Weathermen. These American men and women turned to terrorist bombings when peaceful protests seemed to be doing nothing to bring about an end to the Vietnam War.

Finally, the World Trade Center, destroyed by the September 11 attacks, was actually bombed eight years earlier, probably by al-Qaeda. That bombing resulted in six deaths but no major structural damage to the towers.

Despite these disturbing outbreaks of political violence on American soil, terrorism was never the government's top homeland security priority until September 11, 2001. By successfully attacking the Pentagon and World Trade Center, terrorists demonstrated their ability to strike at the financial and political heart of the nation with devastating effect. Soon, unexpected weapons like box cutters, commercial planes, nail bombs, poisoned water and food, and "dirty bombs" (crude nuclear devices that could spread deadly radiation over a limited area) became the most feared threats. America's intelligence agencies had to adapt to this new reality.

INTELLIGENCE IN THE AGE OF TERROR

The Central Intelligence Agency (CIA) has long been responsible for gathering intelligence about the threats posed by enemy governments. Today, it must also collect all the information available on the plots being hatched by terrorist groups, which are far harder to track and eavesdrop on than are conventional governments. The CIA was founded during World War II and was known as the Office of Strategic Intelligence (OSI). The OSI operated worldwide during the war. Its agents gathered intelligence behind enemy lines, as well as far away from the fighting. They did everything from sabotaging enemy positions to coordinating with resistance groups in occupied countries. After the war, it was obvious that such a foreign intelligence agency was still needed. Since the OSI was created during wartime, however, it needed to be reorganized for peacetime operations. The CIA was the result.

The Federal Bureau of Investigations (FBI) is the CIA's domestic counterpart. It, too, is responsible for gathering intelligence on threats to national security, but it does so within the United States rather than abroad. President Theodore Roosevelt planted the seeds of the bureau in 1908. The need for a federal law enforcement agency arose because of the biased, political nature of law enforcement that existed throughout the nineteenth century. Those who had enough money or connections could often break the law without penalty. The creation of the FBI was supposed to put an end to this corruption while also allowing the US government to enforce the law of the nation across state lines. In this sense, the FBI was like a federal police force.

The FBI is now the most important law enforcement agency combating terrorism within the nation's borders. In October 2001, it gained even more power when Congress passed the Patriot Act. This act allows the government to access far more private information on citizens, makes it easier for the government to tap people's phones or bug their offices and homes, and allows the government to hold illegal immigrants in custody without a trial. Many people have criticized the act for giving the government too much power and access to private information.

SHARING INFORMATION

The Department of Homeland Security will rely upon the intelligence gathered by the FBI and CIA to protect American soil, but it is not a law enforcement or spy agency itself. Instead, the department is designed to prevent terrorist attacks by improving domestic security and, in the event of an attack, to respond quickly and effectively. If the FBI and CIA are at the forefront of the war against terror, the Department of Homeland Security and the various groups included within it play very important supporting roles, such as patrolling the nation's waterways and airports, carefully screening all visitors and temporary residents of the United States, and, if worse comes to worst, providing disaster relief.

The responsibilities assigned to the agencies now included in the Department of Homeland Security have had long, complicated histories

The FBI and CIA inform the Department of Homeland Security about terrorist threats.

of their own. For example, the Federal Emergency Management Agency (FEMA) has been responsible for responding to disasters (both natural and human-made) within the United States since 1979. The Coast Guard has been responsible for protecting the nation's harbors and shores for many years. More recently, the Coast Guard's main concerns have been intercepting drug smugglers and undocumented immigrants. Today, it has the huge responsibility of securing our thousands of miles of shoreline and hundreds of ports from any potential terrorist attacks.

CHAPTER 2

THE PEOPLE KEEPING US SAFE

The idea of homeland security has grown as the United States has evolved from a small group of colonial settlers to the melting pot of more than three hundred million people it is today. For George Washington and the forefathers of the American government, homeland security meant defending the borders against the English. For Abraham Lincoln, it meant defending the country against those in the South who wanted to secede and break the country into two over the issue of slavery. During World War I, it meant fighting a war to prevent political ideals like communism and fascism from reaching American shores.

During World War II, however, homeland security became a major concern. The attack on Pearl Harbor killed over a thousand Americans and destroyed much of the navy's fleet. The Nazis' rapid occupation of most of Europe was also an ominous sign of the future. It proved that a nation's borders could be moved—or erased—overnight. America's

The attack on Pearl Harbor brought homeland security to the forefront of American life.

sudden sense of vulnerability after Pearl Harbor and at the dawn of the nuclear age prompted many anxious calls for greater domestic security.

THE RED SCARE

One of the people who rang the loudest alarms about domestic security was Wisconsin senator Joseph McCarthy. He believed that a group of communist sympathizers was operating within the government. He began witch hunts in the State Department and in different branches

THE SCIENCE OF PROTECTING AMERICA

In order to develop the tools and techniques necessary to combat terrorists and their destructive weapons, the Department of Homeland Security is trying to bring together the latest technology and most talented American scientists. The department's Science and Technology Directorate is responsible for researching and organizing the scientific, engineering, and technological resources of the United States and harnessing them to develop technological tools that will help protect the homeland. Universities, the private sector, and federal laboratories will all be involved in these research and development efforts. The Homeland Security Advanced Research Projects Agency is designed to get an early jump on this research and quickly provide some tools to help fill gaps in homeland defenses.

of the military designed to root out communists. In reality, McCarthy was targeting innocent citizens whose political beliefs were more liberal than his but still firmly democratic and patriotic. Many people's lives were ruined by accusations of communist sympathies. They were often blacklisted, which meant no one would hire them or work with them.

Over time, more and more people began to doubt the truth of Senator McCarthy's accusations. His last shred of credibility was lost when he accused the US Army of harboring communists. This angered President Dwight D. Eisenhower, a former general, and Congress turned its back on McCarthy. His influence quickly diminished. In the end, McCarthy's communist witch hunt was another black eye on the US government's record of protecting its citizens' rights. Unproven claims were once again taken as fact when the public felt threatened. Constitutional protections and the right of due process—the right to a fair trial—had been ignored in the name of homeland security.

A TRAITOR IN THE FBI

Another important figure in the history of domestic security is J. Edgar Hoover. He became the head of the FBI in 1924 and quickly turned it

Legendary FBI head J. Edgar Hoover shaped how the agency operates today.

into the national law enforcement agency it is today. In the 1930s, the agency gained national attention under Hoover for aggressively taking on organized crime. During World War II, the FBI led all intelligence operations inside of the nation's borders. After the war, the bureau continued to direct all domestic intelligence-gathering and began to run background checks on all federal employees in an attempt to prevent foreign agents from entering the government.

As time passed, however, Hoover took his powers with the FBI too far. A fearful and controlling man, he spied and kept files on any American

In 2003, Tom Ridge was appointed as the first secretary of homeland security.

he felt was either a threat to him personally or to the nation. Never before had the US government violated civil liberties so recklessly in order to look into the private lives of citizens. Hoover showed his worst side when it came to the civil rights movement. He continually tried to question the integrity and morals of the Reverend Martin Luther King Jr. In order to try to quash growing sympathy among white Americans for King and the civil rights movement, Hoover even withheld evidence in the trial of several Ku Klux Klan members who had firebombed a church in Birmingham, Alabama, killing four young girls.

Whether or not he really believed that spying on Americans and trying to ruin Dr. King's reputation served the interests of national security, he knew that he could get away with it because few were brave enough to take on the FBI in such a political climate. It was too easy to be branded a traitor or a communist and have one's life ruined as a result.

THE FIRST SECRETARY OF HOMELAND SECURITY

After establishing the Department of Homeland Security, President George W. Bush needed to appoint the department's first secretary, and he chose former Pennsylvania governor Tom Ridge.

Ridge's first job as secretary of homeland security was the very complicated task of figuring out how to fold twenty-two different agencies and 170,000 federal employees into a single, unified government department. Not only was Ridge responsible for the safety of all Americans, he also had to protect the entire nation while creating a brand-new, huge, and untested department. Most important, Ridge had to avoid the errors and excesses of past government officials like Hoover and McCarthy. He had to secure the homeland while protecting Americans' personal freedoms.

CHAPTER 3

WHAT IT TAKES TO KEEP AMERICA SAFE

Although the Department of Homeland Security is fairly new compared to the other cabinet departments, it was created out of twenty-two existing agencies and more than one hundred thousand government employees, all of whom had been working for years to keep America safe. When George W. Bush created the new department, however, he gave it three important directives: to prevent terrorist attacks within the United States; to reduce America's vulnerability to terrorism; and to minimize the damage and lead recovery efforts following any attacks that do occur.

The Department of Homeland Security is composed of four subgroups. They are Information Analysis and Infrastructure Protection; Science and Technology; Border and Transportation Security; and

In November 2002, George W. Bush created the Department of Homeland Security.

Emergency Preparedness and Response. Taken together, these divisions share an enormous variety of responsibilities and perform a wide range of activities.

INFORMATION AND INFRASTRUCTURE

The most important failing of the nation's security system exposed by the September 11 attacks was its inability to use the intelligence that it had gathered about terrorist threats in a way that would help prevent attacks. Early in the process that led to the creation of the Department of Homeland Security, many people were calling for the FBI and the CIA to form the central core of the new department. In this proposed arrangement, the two intelligence agencies would be able to focus their efforts on detecting terrorist threats at home and abroad and share their information. They would be able to use one another's intelligence to detect threats that might otherwise slip through the cracks.

In the end, though, President Bush decided not to include the two intelligence agencies within the new department. White House planners finally decided that making these two agencies part of the Homeland Security Department would have made it more difficult for them to complete their other duties. The FBI is responsible for many federal crimes that have nothing to do with terrorism, such as bank robberies and money laundering. Similarly, the CIA is responsible for intelligence- gathering around the world, much of which is not related to terrorism.

Instead, an intelligence-sharing plan was devised to help the Department of Homeland Security get all of the intelligence that it needs. Through its Office of Information Analysis and Infrastructure Protection, the department receives summary reports from the two agencies. These reports help the department determine the general level of danger posed by terrorists at any given time. The level of danger is announced to the public in the form of the department's color-coded warning system. In colors ranging from green (low risk) to red (severe risk), five different threat levels let Americans know the amount of caution they should use as they go about their daily lives.

Another essential mission of the department's Office of Information Analysis and Infrastructure Protection is to study the vulnerability of

Monitoring possible terrorist activity is only one of the FBI's many duties.

potential targets in the United States and the likelihood of attacks against them. Across the country, there are thousands of potential targets for terrorist attacks. Since terrorism relies on surprise, future terrorist attacks will probably be much different from anything that has been seen before. This leaves the nation's infrastructure—its buildings, roads, railways, power plants, reservoirs, tunnels, and bridges—very vulnerable to terrorist attacks.

There are many possible terrorist targets across the country that were not designed with terrorism in mind. They were not built to withstand the impact of a commercial airliner or a large truck bomb, so their security is of the utmost importance. The Office of Information Analysis and

Infrastructure Protection is responsible for figuring out how vulnerable these sites are and what can be done to make them safer.

SCIENCE AND TECHNOLOGY

The department's Office of Science and Technology is an extremely important part of the overall homeland security strategy. Its main responsibility is to prepare for biological, chemical, or nuclear attacks. It must develop strategies to respond to any of these types of attacks if they do occur. It is also responsible for developing methods to monitor and prevent the smuggling of such weapons into the United States. To fulfill both these goals, the office conducts a lot of research. This research includes finding vaccines to fight the effects of biological and chemical weapons; preparing hospitals to be able to treat victims of biological, chemical, or nuclear attacks; and developing technology that can detect these types of weapons at our borders.

The technology side of the Science and Technology Office works to develop new ways to respond to terrorism. It seeks to develop new devices that can detect weapons of mass destruction at our borders as well as equipment that can halt or minimize the damage of a biological, chemical, or nuclear attack. Many independent businesses, funded in part by the Department of Homeland Security, have attempted to address the security failures that allowed the September 11 terrorist attacks, as well as the equipment failures that made the response to the attacks ineffective. For example, one company designed vehicles equipped to communicate with any type of radio. If these vehicles had been in use on September 11, 2001, hundreds of firefighters might still be

Homeland Security's forensic lab focuses on handling biological, chemical, and nuclear threats.

alive today. Another company designed a small scanner that can tell if a passport or driver's license is real or not so that known terrorists cannot use fake identification.

BORDERS AND IMMIGRATION

Another extremely important job of the Department of Homeland Security is its role in border and transportation security. All of the September 11 hijackers entered the country in the two years before the attacks. Most of them entered only days before. It was the failings of airport security policies and personnel that allowed nineteen men to board four flights armed with box cutters. The borders of the United States are vast. The two shared with Canada and Mexico are a combined 6,500 miles (10,460 kilometers) long. Furthermore, five hundred million people enter and leave the United States every year. There are so many different points of entry along these borders and at the nation's hundreds of international airports and ports that policing this enormous territory is an extremely difficult and challenging job.

One of the newer initiatives of the Border and Transportation Security Office is the Office of Biometric Identity Management program. With this program, the nation's borders quickly became more organized. Many of the September 11 hijackers were living in the country on

Fingerprint scanners help track international visitors to the United States.

expired visas. If the INS had been keeping better track of them, these men may have been sent back to their home countries before they had a chance to go through with their plan.

Now, when foreign citizens enter the country, they are kept track of from the minute they apply for a visa until the moment they leave the country. At the borders, they are electronically fingerprinted and photographed so that the border officers can match up the person leaving the country with the name they have on their computer screen. All official actions, such as hospital visits and appointments at immigration offices within the United States, are kept track of as well. The idea behind the program is to gather as much information as possible about the individual attempting to enter the country in order to make an educated decision about whether that person should be allowed in.

EMERGENCY RESPONSE

The Office of Emergency Preparedness and Response is the fourth office within the Department of Homeland Security. It is concerned with the "first responders"—the police officers, firefighters, and emergency medical personnel who are the first people to respond to any disaster. The events of September 11 showed how important it is to be prepared to respond to terrorist

THE SECRET SERVICE

When the Department of Homeland Security was created in 2002, the Secret Service—the agency devoted to protecting the president, vice president, their families, and visiting foreign leaders—became a part of the new group. In order to protect the president, the Secret Service seeks help from other federal, state, and local law enforcement agencies. For example, when the president is working at the White House, the Secret Service Uniformed Division, the Washington Metropolitan Police Department, and the US Park Police patrol the streets and parks nearby to prevent any unwanted intruders from gaining access to the White House grounds. When the president travels away from Washington, a team of Secret Service agents arrives several days earlier and works with the host city and state law enforcement and public safety officials to jointly establish the security measures needed to protect the president.

Better communication systems could have saved the lives of many first responders on 9/11.

attacks. The New York City Fire Department was not ready to deal with a disaster of that type or magnitude. The firefighters' instructions had to be radioed from the fire chief through each individual firehouse's radio system. The time lag that this caused doomed many firefighters in the World Trade Center. When it became clear that the towers were about to collapse, evacuation orders were sent out but did not reach many of them in time.

First responders have to know exactly how to deal with any medical issues if they are to save victims' lives and limit any further damage. Understanding this need, the Office of Emergency Preparedness and

Response trains first responders all across the country and provides the money needed to bring police and fire departments, hospitals, and their equipment up to code. A government agency with over twenty years of experience with emergency and disaster response—the Federal Emergency Management Agency (FEMA)—has been folded into the Office of Emergency Preparedness and Response. FEMA will continue to be the first federal organization to arrive at the scene of every type of disaster, from terrorist attacks and train wrecks to wildfires and floods. It responds to disasters by providing information and advice to local officials. Perhaps more important, FEMA also brings supplies and money to aid in disaster relief and recovery.

CHAPTER 4

PROTECTING AMERICA'S FUTURE

More than fifteen years after its creation, the Department of Homeland Security remains an important part of the US government. In recent years, the department has been tasked with tackling not only terrorists trying to enter the country from abroad, but homegrown terrorists inspired by those abroad. Since 2014, there have been a multitude of attacks on American soil, from small-scale shootings to much larger attacks, and each one has made it clear why the Department of Homeland Security remains essential to keeping Americans safe.

ISIS

The Islamic State, frequently referred to as ISIS, is a radical Islamic terror organization that formed in 2014, after American forces left Iraq following nearly a decade of war.

Keeping the United States safe is an ongoing, evolving mission of homeland security.

While the Islamic State focuses much of its terror activities on those living within the borders the group established in the Middle East, many people around the world have been inspired by the group and have chosen to act on that inspiration by attacking Americans across the country.

In December 2015, a married couple shot and killed fourteen people in San Bernadino, California. They were allegedly inspired to commit the murders by ISIS. In January 2016, a man shot a Philadelphia, Pennsylvania, police officer in the name of ISIS. In June 2016, a man inspired by the Islamic State killed fifty people and injured dozens during a terror attack on the Pulse nightclub in Orlando, Florida. And in October 2017, a man drove his car onto a crowded New York City

The shooter at the Pulse nightclub attack in Orlando claimed an allegiance to ISIS.

bike path, killing eight people and injuring at least a dozen more, all in the name of ISIS. And these are only a few of the many attacks that have taken place in recent years.

These attacks on American soil are what are referred to as lone-wolf attacks, attacks that are carried out by individuals without direction from a larger group but inspired by the hate that group promotes.

As the Department of Homeland Security has learned in recent years, it's incredibly difficult to predict the actions of lone wolves. Many of these attackers discover their terrorist leanings online, where they have the gift of anonymity. They can search for advice and inspiration for their attacks without anyone ever knowing and can make contact with terror leaders through social media without ever sharing their real name.

SECURITY CONCERNS OF THE FUTURE

While ISIS has taken up much of the Department of Homeland Security's time over the past five years, there are other groups that pose as great a threat in America. One of the biggest concerns of the department today is white supremacy and white nationalist groups like the Ku Klux Klan and neo-Nazi groups.

In 2015, Dylann Roof attacked and killed numerous black citizens at a church in Charleston, South Carolina. Roof was later discovered to share many beliefs with white supremacists, which are believed to have inspired his choice of victims.

In the following two years, white supremacist groups staged marches and protests across America. A young woman, Heather Heyer, was attending a counterprotest of a right-wing nationalist march when she was run down and killed by a man who believed in white nationalism, the ideology that believes white men and women are superior to people of color and that there should be a whites-only homeland in the United States.

SOCIAL MEDIA

Terrorists have found it incredibly easy to spread their messages of hate through social media. By creating anonymous accounts on websites like Facebook and Twitter, Islamic State supporters can share information with one another and encourage each other to stage attacks close to home. The man who attacked pedestrians in New York City in October 2017 was inspired to commit that act by videos he found posted online. Unfortunately, it's nearly impossible for the Department of Homeland Security to stop the spread of these social media messages. For every terror message removed from social media, many more spring up, and because the accounts that post them are often anonymous and are created and deleted within hours or days, there's no way to prevent the posters. It's also impossible to stop the spread of the messages because one post can be shared hundreds or thousands of times in a matter of minutes, so even if it or the account that posted it are deleted, it has already reached its target audience.

The internet provides a powerful platform for terrorist ideologies to spread.

Prior to Heyer's murder in August 2017, the Department of Homeland Security, in partnership with the FBI, produced a memo that declared that white supremacists "likely will continue to pose a threat of lethal violence over the next year." The internal report, published in May 2017, found that white supremacists "were responsible for 49 homicides in 26 attacks from 2000 to 2016 … more than any other domestic extremist movement."

CONCLUSION

In the coming years, the Department of Homeland Security will have to face not only growing security threats from American citizens and terrorists from abroad, but will need to navigate a new technological environment that makes it increasingly easy for these terrorists to plot and scheme in anonymity, making it harder than ever for security personnel to prevent attacks before they happen.

While trying to stop terrorism at home, the department will also need to work to ensure that everyday Americans don't have their rights violated simply because they fall into a particular demographic. The secretary of homeland security will need to make sure that Muslims—both immigrants and natural-born citizens—aren't profiled and stripped of their rights the way Japanese Americans were following the attack on Pearl Harbor. He or she will also need to make sure that not all politically conservative citizens are considered terror threats, even if they share beliefs with white nationalists. It will be important for the department to help citizens retain their rights of free speech, even if that speech is hateful and similar in content and kind to the speech of terrorists.

The freedoms America provides its citizens make it harder for the Department of Homeland Security to do its job, but it's those freedoms that the department is tasked with protecting. As more threats arise, it will be up to the department and its leaders to keep Americans and their freedoms flourishing while finding new ways to stop those who wish to prevent Americans from enjoying their freedoms here at home.

Chronology

1908   The Federal Bureau of Investigation (FBI) is established.

December 7, 1941   The US Navy base at Pearl Harbor in Hawaii is attacked by the Japanese air force. War is immediately declared on Japan.

1947   The Central Intelligence Agency (CIA) is established.

May 1978   The Unabomber, Ted Kaczynski, begins an eighteen-year terror campaign when he sends his first mail bomb to a technical school in New York.

1979   The Federal Emergency Management Agency (FEMA) is established.

April 19, 1995   The Murrah Federal Building in Oklahoma City is bombed by Timothy McVeigh, who is later convicted and given the death sentence.

May 4, 1998   Ted Kaczynski is sentenced to more than four life terms.

August 7, 1998   Al-Qaeda blows up two American embassies in Nairobi, Kenya, and Dar es Salaam, Tanzania; 224 people are killed.

October 12, 2000   Osama bin Laden bombs the USS *Cole* in Yemen's Aden harbor, killing seventeen American sailors.

September 11, 2001   Terrorists hijack four airplanes. Two of the planes are flown into the World Trade Center, one is flown into the Pentagon near Washington, DC, and the fourth crashes in a Pennsylvania field.

September 20, 2001 President Bush establishes the Office of Homeland Security, which will advise the president on security matters. Pennsylvania governor Tom Ridge is named to head the office.

October 26, 2001 President Bush signs the USA Patriot Act.

November 19, 2001 The Transportation Security Administration is created to address problems in airport security.

June 6, 2002 President Bush announces the creation of the cabinet-level Department of Homeland Security. Tom Ridge becomes the department's first secretary.

March 1, 2003 The last of the agencies to be transferred into the Department of Homeland Security are integrated, and the department becomes a fully functioning agency for the first time. This includes the Immigration and Naturalization Service (INS).

May 12, 2003 The first national homeland security drill—TopOff II—is run.

2014 ISIS, a radical Islamic terror organization, is formed.

June 17, 2015 Dylann Roof, an American white supremacist, kills nine African Americans during a prayer service at Emanuel African Methodist Episcopal Church in Charleston, South Carolina.

December 2, 2015 Syed Rizwan Farook and Tashfeen Malik, husband and wife, kill fourteen people in a mass shooting in San Bernardino, California. It is declared a terrorist attack as ISIS allegedly inspired the couple.

January 7, 2016 Edward Archer shoots Jesse Harnett, a Philadelphia police officer, repeatedly in the arm. Archer later reveals his loyalty to ISIS.

June 12, 2016   Omar Mateen, a twenty-nine-year-old security guard, kills forty-nine people and injures forty-eight others in a terrorist attack/hate crime that takes place in Pulse, a gay nightclub in Orlando, Florida.

August 12, 2017   Heather Heyer is killed when James Alex Fields Jr. crashes his car into an anti–white supremacist rally in Charlottesville, Virginia.

October 31, 2017   Twenty-nine-year-old Sayfullo Saipov, an Uzbek citizen, intentionally crashes his truck into a bike path in Manhattan, killing eight people while shouting "Allauh Akbar," meaning "God is great," in Arabic.

GLOSSARY

cabinet A council of chief advisers to a head of state.

cabinet-level department A government office headed by a key adviser to a head of state, such as the president of the United States.

civil rights The legal rights of a citizen, protecting him or her from the oppression or injustice of government and individuals.

facilitate To make a process easier.

federal Of or relating to the central governing authority in a nation made up of several states or territories.

hostile Of or belonging to an enemy; unfriendly.

immigrant Citizen or resident who has come from a foreign country.

infrastructure The support system of a city or country that allows it to function, such as the sanitation system, power plants, water pipelines, bridges, tunnels, highways, and railways.

initiative A course of action.

intelligence Information about a threat or enemy.

merit The rights and wrongs of a case.

sabotage To intentionally destroy or damage something.

scheme A plan to put a particular idea into effect.

smuggle To sneak illegal items or persons through the borders of a nation.

supremacist Someone who favors one group of people above another, usually on the basis of race or gender.

terrorism The act of attacking a group of innocent people in order to cause fear or death often carried out to gain attention for a small group's cause or belief.

Further Reading

Books

Haney, Philip, and Art Moore. *See Something, Say Nothing: A Homeland Security Officer Exposes the Government's Submission to Jihad.* Washington, DC: WND Books, 2016.

Orr, Tamra. *September 11 and Terrorism in America.* Ann Arbor, MI: Cherry Lake Publishing, 2017.

White, Jonathan R. *Terrorism and Homeland Security.* Boston, MA: Cengage Learning, 2017.

Websites

Central Intelligence Agency Office of Public Affairs
https://www.cia.gov/about-cia/history-of-the-cia
The Central Intelligence Agency focuses on gathering information overseas about potential threats to the United States.

Department of Homeland Security
https://www.dhs.gov
The Department of Homeland Security is a cabinet department that handles terrorism and border security, among other duties.

Federal Bureau of Investigation
https://www.fbi.gov/about
The FBI is a law enforcement agency that investigates both domestic and international crimes relating to the United States.

Federal Emergency Management Agency
https://www.fema.gov/about-agency Bibliography
Providing disaster relief and supporting recovery efforts are the chief tasks of the Federal Emergency Management Agency.

BIBLIOGRAPHY

"About CIA." CIA Homepage. Retrieved December 2017. https://www. cia.gov/about-cia.

"About DHS." DHS Homepage. Retrieved December 2017. https://www. dhs.gov/about-dhs.

"About FBI." FBI Homepage. Retrieved December 2017. https://www.fbi. gov/about.

Bernstein, Nina. "Relatives of Interned Japanese-Americans Side with Muslims." *New York Times,* April 3, 2007. http://www.nytimes. com/2007/04/03/nyregion/03detain.html.

Buncombe, Andrew. "Heather Heyer Was Buried in Secret Grave to Protect It from Neo-Nazis After Charlottesville, Reveals Mother." *Independent,* December 15, 2017. http://www.independent.co.uk/ news/world/americas/heather-heyer-grave-secret-hide-nazis-charlot-tesville-attack-mother-reveals-a8113056.html.

Cobb, Jelani. "Inside the Trial of Dylann Roof." *New Yorker,* February 6, 2017. https://www.newyorker.com/magazine/2017/02/06/ inside-the-trial-of-dylann-roof.

FBI. "East African Embassy Bombings." FBI Famous Cases & Criminals. Retrieved December 2017 (https://www.fbi.gov/history/famous-cases/ east-african-embassy-bombings).

Felter, Claire, and Danielle Renwick. "The U.S. Immigration Debate." *Council on Foreign Relations,* September 6, 2017. https://www.cfr.org/ backgrounder/us-immigration-debate-0.

"FEMA History." FEMA Homepage. Retrieved December 2017. http://www.fema.gov/about/history.shtm.

"History of the FBI." FBI Homepage. Retrieved December 2017. http://www.fbi.gov/libref/historic/history/historymain.htm.

Kephart, Janice. "US-VISIT Is Now the Office of Biometric Identity Management (and That's a Good Thing)." Center for Immigration Studies, April 15, 2013. https://cis.org/Kephart/USVISIT-Now-Office-Biometric-Identity-Management-and-Thats-Good-Thing.

Khedery, Ali. "How Isis Came to Be." *Guardian,* August 22, 2014. https://www.theguardian.com/world/2014/aug/22/syria-iraq-incubators-isis-jihad.

"National Strategy for Homeland Security." White House, July 2002. Retrieved July 2003. http://www.whitehouse.gov/homeland/book.

Pérez-Péna, Richard, and Michael S. Schmidt. "F.B.I. Treating San Bernardino Attack as Terrorism Case." *New York Times,* December 4, 2015. https://www.nytimes.com/2015/12/05/us/tashfeen-malik-islamic-state.html.

"USS Cole Bombing." 9/11 Memorial & Museum. Retrieved December 2017. https://www.911memorial.org/uss-cole-bombing.

INDEX